ITSELF

WESLEYAN POETRY

I T

Rae Armantrout

S E L F

Wesleyan University Press ⌣ Middletown, Connecticut

Wesleyan University Press
Middletown CT 06459
www.wesleyan.edu/wespress
© 2015 Rae Armantrout
Manufactured in the United States of America
Designed by Mindy Basinger Hill
Typeset in Minion Pro

Wesleyan University Press is a member
of the Green Press Initiative. The paper used
in this book meets their minimum requirement for
recycled paper.

Library of Congress Cataloging-in-Publication Data

Armantrout, Rae, 1947–
[Poems. Selections]
Itself / Rae Armantrout.
       pages;   cm. —(Wesleyan poetry series)
ISBN 978-0-8195-7467-1 (hardcover: acid-free paper) —
ISBN 978-0-8195-7568-8 (ebook)
I. Title.
PS3551. R455A6 2015
811'.54—dc23 2014034434

This project is supported in part by an award
from the National Endowment for the Arts.

5   4   3   2   1

The animals themselves occupied only

the last and largest chamber; the rest were

filled with air. The walls between the chambers,

known as septa, were fantastically elaborate,

folded into intricate ruffles.

ELIZABETH KOLBERT
The Sixth Extinction: An Unnatural History

CONTENTS

ACKNOWLEDGMENTS

The author wishes to thank the editors of the following journals and anthologies:

Anthologies

The Best American Poetry 2014, Scribner, ed. David Lehman and Terrance Hayes

The Sonnets: Translating and Rewriting Shakespeare, Telephone Books, ed. Sharmilla Cohen and Paul Legault

Journals

1913 A Journal of Forms, 580 Split, Academy of American Poets Poem-a-Day, *The Baffler, Blackbox Manifold, Boston Review, Burnside Review, Cambridge Literary Review, Chicago Review, Columbia Poetry Review, Conjunctions*, Dusie Blog, *The Fiddlehead, Grey Magazine, The Hat, Jacket2, Lana Turner, London Review of Books, Manor House Quarterly, N/A, The Nation, The New Yorker, The New York Times Sunday Review* (April 15, 2012), *Noö, Plume, Poetry Magazine, Public Space, The Salzberg Review, Wave Composition, West Wind Review*

one ITSELF

CHIRALITY

If I didn't need
to do anything,
would I?

Would I oscillate
in two
or three dimensions?

Would I summon
a beholder

and change chirality
for "him?"

A massless particle
passes through the void
with no resistance.

Ask what it means
to pass through the void.

Ask how it differs
from not passing.

A CONCEIT

Local anchors list the ways
viewers might enjoy tomorrow.

One says, "Get some great . . . ," but
that seems like a stretch.

The other snickers, meaning,
"Where were you going with that?"

Like you thought

~

Like you could defend
vanity

in the sense of
idle conceit,

vacuous self-
absorption,

doing whatever
it takes to

whatever
because,

really.

~

As if to say,

"Conceit
is the vacuum energy."

Because you dodge
yourselves
by branching,

(expelling particles
of light).

Because you split
no-difference,

sights strike me
as

～

A muscular gray cat
trots

along the top of
the cinderblock wall

separating my couch
from the supermarket.

～

25% say, "That's
just it, Pam!"

～

I take these
white streaks

of truck

glimpsed
between branches

to be blossoms.

INDUCTION

What's the take-away?

~

Carrying plastic buckets,
an old couple stroll
along the high-water mark.

~

The rapture: such
wings of cloud —

sleeves of fire
as previously noted.

~

Passing obliquely
through the interface,

desire is refracted.

~

Low sun illuminates
a row of amber
pill bottles,

half full.

CONCLUSION

1

A man is upset for many years
because he's heard
that information is destroyed
in a black hole.

Question: What does this man mean
by "information"?

The example given
is of a cry for help,

but this is accompanied
by the image of a toy space ship,
upended,

and is thus
not to be taken seriously.

The man recovers his peace of mind
when he ceases to believe
in passing through,

when he becomes convinced
that the lost information

is splattered
on the event

horizon.

2

The detective is the new mime.

She acts out understanding
the way a mime
climbs an invisible wall.

～

It's because our senses
are so poor that,

on CSI,
the investigators
stand stock-still,

boulders in a stream,

while a crowd
pours around them.

They pan
in slow motion, reminding us
of cameras,

then focus
with inhuman clarity

on the pattern of cracks
in a wall.

3

God's fractal
stammer

pleasures us
again.

PITCH

1

Beautiful,
the way the partita

progresses and retreats
(repeats?).

This node
virtually branching

on two "sides,"

without haste or
seeming intent,

almost reluctantly,
in fact,
almost "sending regrets."

2

Long-Term Technologies
has made these

fully nuanced,
self-reflexive stanzas —

sliver echoes —

"Silver Acres"—

widely available

to the shelter-in-place
public.

PRICE POINTS

On a traffic island, a man waves his arms
as if conducting music,
and takes bows.

He gets no points
for originality,

plus we're sick
of being represented.

The tabloids are right.

An appearance
requires scandal.

To be notable,
something must appear
instead

of what?

◞

This spike reflects.

◞

This spike
reflects
global demand
for food
products.

DIFFERENCE

1

Catch us up
to where we are
today —

these pants!
this hair!

~

It's been a good year
for unique, differentiated products.

~

I'm more interested
in quarks:

up and down,
bottom and top,

simple units
of meaning.

2

If self-love
were a mirage,

it would decorate
distance,

shimmer over
others' eyes,

evaporate
on contact

EDEN

1

About can mean near
or nearly.

A book can be about something

or I can be about
to do a thing
and then refrain.

To refrain is to stop yourself.

A refrain
is a repeated phrase.

2

This table is an antique
from the early Machine Age.
The indented
circle within a circle
motif
which appears
at three-inch intervals
around the base
may be a nod
to craftsmanship
or may be a summary
dismissal of same.

It is *charming*
in its mute simplicity.

3

People will ask, "Why should we care about this unattractive character?"
despite the fact that turning yourself into an admirable character
has been considered gauche for as long as I can recall.

The word "transparent" is often affixed to such efforts
while the mystification surrounding the unflattering self-portrait
at least provides some cover.

Now someone will say, "You don't need cover
unless you're standing naked at a window
shouting, 'Look up here!'"

SONNET 3

after Wm. Shakespeare

Your dad told me to tell you
how good you look to him right now.
Check yourself out. (I'm sure you do.)
You're a very pretty boy.
But the thing is, that won't last.
Have you ever seen a pert old man?
An insouciant septuagenarian?
I thought not. They're invisible.
And you'll be invisible too!
What will your dad have
to look at then? Do you think growth
rebounds each year? Wrong!
It has to be outsourced. Sublet.
Get with the program.
Your dad will be watching.

ITSELF

I work it
until sweetness

rises
of itself,

then arcs across,
unfurling petals,

and is gone.

⁓

On television hundreds
of albino crabs
scuffle
over one steam vent.

⁓

I know you're dreaming
things I haven't dreamed,

wouldn't. But that's part
of your costume

like your extra
appendages.

ROOMS

To be human is to count

the present

among one's possessions.

~

A sparsely furnished house

appears in my dreams —

or *is* my dream

since nothing happens

except my walking

room to room, surprised,

discomfited.

~

One can't have

just one

experience.

(There will be

no one

to own it.)

BIVOUAC

1

Their knees touched at night
when they lay on their sides.

The pressure of the bony plates
was a wall

or the pressure was union.

She had relaxed
against it.

2

Meaning is sensed relation.

The body's sensed relation
to space?

A body's well-being
in relation
to an environment.

She ripped a feather
from her tail
and placed it in the nest.

She discarded this
and extracted a second

MATERIAL

Oh, you're wearing the gold one.

That's my favorite,
to be honest.

The gun metal is all gone.

~

Packet.
Pocket.
Point.

For us to consist
of infinitesimal points

of want
and not

makes a lot of sense.

(For a point to consist
of the array

of its own
possible locations

For locations to consist

For "consist" to consist
of a pair
of empty pockets)

~

Here, you try it on.

FLO

1

In this spot for insurance,
a savvy young agent,
almost pretty,
says "Go Big Money!"
to a subordinate
tap-dancing
in a dollar-sign costume
in front of her confused/
bemused clients.

This agent, Flo,
who is above it all
but enthusiastic too
like the Dalai Lama,
has become/
is becoming
an American icon.

2

What I first saw
as tiny, novel
fireplaces scattered about
the living room floor,
I now see as the house gone
up in flames —
but this is wrong
because "first"
was part of "now"
from the very start.

THE NEW IRONY

1

In the new irony,
particulars
are overdetermined,

dripping context,

while the big picture
remains obscure:

1940s pinup girls
in Brownie uniforms,

sizes too small,
rush

toward a blazing
office tower

so that rescue,
porn,
and nostalgia

converge.

2

It was my understanding
that things would be
muffled,

remote

SPONSOR

We drove to the slough and walked briefly
along the uneven path.

There are plants here
you see nowhere else,
you said.

Pickle weed? Duck weed?

Branching pipettes.

⁓

Among twenty brown hills
the only moving thing
was the Coca-Cola truck.

THE MATTER

The remote
is for later,

as I often
tell myself.

～

Is it possible to speak
of rules
without picturing
the mouth of God?

He said, "You must go
everywhere

and you should take
the shortcut."

The angels responded
at once,

as one?

Thus they are known
as messengers —

though they bring
nothing
but their gowns.

The rest of us
stand still,

flummoxed

by the hostility
of pronouns

TWO AND TWO

1

If one travels to the old country
and finds it

there,

she's thrilled.
Surprised.

If there
and here
can be made

to coincide

what else
might not be

possible?

2

The tapir. The tape worm.

The question. The lepton.

3

But If *what*

is "a mode of
oscillating,"

then *how*

is unaccounted

            for

PERSONHOOD

1

Imagine the recent dead
gathered in a parking lot
or lobby

wearing Victorian clothes
to distinguish themselves
from the passersby —

a flash mob .

They can't take themselves
or one another
seriously. It's hard

to hold on
to an idea

2

Clearly, each
orange parasol

of poppy,

having opened,
is one.

But effort is not
cumulative.

It figures
second
to second.

A self
is a lagging

indicator

FRIENDS

1

Peace be upon
the transparent maroon curtain
and the chesty air-conditioning unit
spilling yellow foam from between its ribs,
side-swiped by sun
so that shadows
of the window bars around it
in the shape of two
Valentine's Day hearts,
one perched upside down
on top of its mate,
can grow sharp.

2

In the next seat
a dentist tells her friend
she is reading *Rent Boy to the Stars*
and a book on reincarnation.

3

"I'm all used up,"
I tell myself,
"all gone"
like that was some new
kind of luxury —
one I could afford!

THE COUPLE

I compare notes
and snip.

More matches!

You. You
know it's

a very fine line.

⁓

If I
am really speaking to you

from inside
the echo chamber

where you float,
then something's wrong.

⁓

Ka-Ching!

I grow a bony plate
around you.

Now,
what do you think?

As one
may be relieved
by the myriad
marigold faces
held aloft
beside the freeway —
their articulation —

and, too,
by the rush
of notes
following their own
likenesses
in these headlong
phrases

Relieved of what?
Relieved of what?

FUNDAMENTALS

Why is it that
for it

to be in-
finitely large

is terrific,
but to be

infinitely small
is just

unthinkable?

The thought
of a smaller

bit inside
each bit

goes nowhere
still

has symmetry
going on

and on
about it.

Then there's our model
in which

the fundamentals
are sound,

impenetrable nubs

two MEMBRANE

MEMBRANE

When she hugged him
I wanted her
to hug me too because,
if she didn't,
I would have to wonder
about that, whereas,
before, I would have been happy
with a friendly word and,
after a slight hesitation,
she did
wrap her arms around me

　　　~

　　　ion
　　　selection
　　　channel
　　　membrane

　　　~

Put simply,
the snake told Eve

that gods
(people)

do things for reasons,

reasons they may not
admit,

but which she should
learn to intuit.

Once this thought
had been set loose,

(once she had compared
herself . . .)

there would be no end
of that

KEEPERS

1

On "Buried Alive,"
possessions can't be lost

or found.
They can't be exchanged.

They're negotiated

as one negotiates
a landfill.

2

In the militarized evening,
Boeing

touts its service
to "our troops." We're shown

soldiers pinned down.
One is strapped

to a pallet —
ready for take-off?

3

In the currency market,
I'm the judge

of a talent show
or beauty pageant

in which the contestants
are moments

of my life. None
is good enough

to keep

POEM

Now our bodies
are two scoops of ice cream
beginning to melt.

"Now" can't begin.

⁓

You are not asleep
now. Now does not exist
when you're asleep.

Now means, "Now
do something!"

I can turn over
in my sleep. I
can dream.

⁓

Now is when
you can *choose*
to do something.

Then which comes now,
doing or choosing?

⁓

Skirting
the edge of

what can,
could have been

meant

ALIGNMENT

She knew it was a bad idea
to ask how he was doing,
or to tell him how she was,
but she *could* draw him out
on the logical flaws
in a film they had both
disliked.

She wants to make
their suspicions
align,
face forward
like two doves on a wire —
good pupils.

She wakes up
when the girl hides
in the old woman's house
so now
either the madman will kill her
or nothing further will occur.

HABITAT

Habitat-themed enclosure.

Zen-inflected mug.

~

Around the block
dogs bark at absence.

THE WAIT

A story deals with distance;
how it can be crossed.

There will be dangerous animals
in the form of questions.

Some Jack of Clubs
will have hit upon an answer,

beguiled hunger,

continued.

⁓

I can't wait to start out
dreaming (thinking).

This means I wait.
Consciousness is so boring

with its identification
of noises
in the dark,

its taxonomies
of grinding.

⁓

In my dreams,
feelings are tacked on
to shapes.

One or the other
must be an afterthought.

Together they make
an awkward animal.

This is also true
when I'm awake,

but for that, of course,
I am not responsible.

OCCURRENCE

Here's something about me.

I get up when sleep
becomes unbearable,
when dreams repeat themselves,
minor variations
on a randomly selected theme.

I go to bed
when consciousness becomes unbearable,
when the house repeats itself
and the television offers
to think for me.

Lay-offs accelerate
turn-around.

Aliens may try
to communicate with us
using black holes.

Here is what we know
about God.

If we are made in God's image,
God is impatient
without really knowing
what He wishes
would occur.

END USER

What do I have to say
to myself?

My username
is invalid.

∽

Pain concentrates:

a continuous signal
that consumes
the receiver.

∽

The belief that nature
is God's speech:

small tomato
cysts

appear

on shingle twigs
under bow-tie leaves.

∽

So when water
or shadows

are going over
"the same ground?"

~

"Made any money though?"
one asks

and both
laugh loudly.

LOOP

Curled up in bed,
I'm young
in the old way.

One
continuous stroke

without lifting
the pen

as if

"stem, tendril,
stem, tendril"

were the words
of a commandment.

My next
elliptical loops

read "Praise."

Word

deciphered

at a snail's
pace

GEOGRAPHY

1

Touch each chakra
in turn and say,

"Nothing shocks me."

2

Watching bombs fall
on Syria,

we feel serious,

occupied,

not preoccupied
as we were

previously.

3

"Makes me end
where I begun,"

wrote John Donne,

turning love
into geometry.

PERSISTENCE

What if one loves
what she thinks of as
her former self
in what she takes
to be another's
eyes?

~

The celebration of false wealth —
or "Cold Light" —

is my favorite.

Blue glittering
fruit,

as if frost
might be our guest.

Countless small
white bulbs

behind cutout crystals.

~

The persistence
of desire

in mind
after desire

has or hasn't
been fulfilled:

the "other world"

PLACE MARK

Shiva arms
of the potato vine

so eager to unleash
this bloom

they can spare only a few
dark leaves.

～

Tip
of the thrust

only,

like a distant
spark

chipped off

and marking
space.

～

"I feel it,"
I said

and you came.

BELIEVING

1

When did you first learn
that the bursts

of color and sound
were intended for you?

When did you unlearn this?

2

Believing yourself
to have a secret identity
can be a sign
of madness.

On the other hand,
the lack
of a secret identity
can lead to depression.

Many have found it useful
to lie down
as men
believing themselves
to be little girls

or as girls
believing themselves
to be mermaids
stranded
in their own bodies.

HEAD

1

You just feel wrong
so you convert

one neutron
to a proton,

emit beta radiation.

2

You try
not to squirm,

to cancel
yourself out,

still, in dreams
you narrate

each discharge
in the first person.

3

As if you were
banging your head

on every beach
in frustration

CONTROL

We are learning to control our thoughts,
to set obtrusive thoughts aside.

It takes an American
to do really big things.

Often I have no thoughts to push against.

It's lonely in a song
about outer space.

When I don't have any thoughts,
I want one!

A close-up reveals
that she has chosen

a plastic soap dish
in the shape of a giant sea turtle.

Can a thought truly be mine
if I am not currently thinking it?

There are two sides
to any argument;

one arm
in each sleeve.

~

Maybe I am always meditating,
if by that you mean

searching for a perfect
stranger.

DIFFICULTY

It's difficult
not to be sentimental

about the sun
at first,

or when it first
slides out

from between
clouds

and we say it has
"returned."

But I should back up
and explain

to the alien
doctors

that we know it's wrong
to be sentimental.

It means you're too easy
on yourself

or you're an easy
mark, maybe,

a pushover,

and we're brighter
than that.

Look there!

RITUALS

1

In this now ancient ritual
a succession of young women

are saucy,

which is to say they name
common objects and relations

as if they had mastered them
but shouldn't.

Each receives false approbation.

2

As Xmas sells winter
to its prisoners.

As warmth
feels like love;

and love is warmth
only more capricious.

Fingers uncurl.

Organs expand
and rise

toward a surface
that must never

be broken.

THE TIMES .

1

By "classical"
we mean the age

when the woods were haunted
by near misses,

not-quite girls
seen from the corner

of whose eye,
leaving branches

trembling
or strangely still.

2

The journals for sale here
no longer pretend

to be made from
dead animals;

now it's
strips of newsprint

and straw
that are retro.

3

It's the flimsiness
of the petals,

the way they're always
open-shut

though nobody
has seen them

move

EVIDENCE

Brittle, elevated
track

a snail laid down
on that flagstone,

its mysterious swerves.

　　　～

When the cup tilts,
my eye appears
at the bottom,

placid, singular.

　　　～

I've "added a window
to the world."

Believe it?

Look at these
convincing shards.

　　　～

The flagstone
itself,

a jagged blue-
pink dawn

slab

HOUSES

What's lacking
in the film version?

Worry bead lists,
descriptions

of imaginary feudal
sigils.

⁓

Someone says it's an ugly
universe with its

37 families
of subatomic particles.

Sums should be evenly
divisible.

⁓

Platonic forms:

floors and hallways
built of living

ants

ALL SOULS

Pallid, thin-skinned
potatoes bunched
like grapes
on yellow stems.

~

I can't remember
my mother

or

This is not the mother
I remember.

~

When asked
if she's frightened,

the raped child
whispers

that she is afraid
of ghosts.

FUNCTIONS

1

We inquire about heaven
as we might
about a nursing home.

Will I get email there?

Will I have insights

and someone
to be pleased with them?

Will that person
be faking it?

Will she be under orders?

Will my words
seem foreign?

2

"Twee, twee!"
some sound insists.

OUR WORLD

We'd been tweaking
the poignancy

of small plots
for how long?

    ~

We needed space,

perceived distance
between thing and statement,

as if irony,
inflated,
might be a whole new globe.

    ~

The "Unique Cab"
is a yellow sedan.

More?

Say the window decals
on the minivan

are two small skulls
with bows floating above.

    ~

In our world,
scissors fly

around unheld, trim
Cinderella's evening gown;

and freshly released
virions

self-assemble
inside the host

EPISODES

1

Two children travel to Australia
in an instant
with the aid of a magical dog,
really a witch,
and a book on the animals
of the outback
which race past —
as soon as the kids appear —
followed by predators
that the boy and girl
can name.

2

Hot comedy: "God of Carnage."

Having trouble viewing this?

3

In the opener,
a ramified tube

speaks
of itself, to itself,

saying, "Not bad."

THE PULL

1

Inspiration is 98%
pulling a trope
from one medium
into another so that
a drop
of its substance
is wrung out.

We sustain ourselves
on this.

2

Like a ventriloquist's dummy,
you told us

that the young and beautiful
should breed.

3

Each skittering in,
thin and bright,

across the length
of its own ghost,

which slides back,
sighing.

Breathe

I discovered you at eleven, listening
to the Everly Brothers
singing "Dream, Dream, Dream."

Whenever I want you,

longing puts distance
between us

and a supposed object —

a space awash
in possibility.

⁓

On an obscure track,
Mick's minor key falsetto

intoning, "You, you, you, you"
until the word means nothing,

anything.

⁓

You sparrow fluttering
between here and here.

You reverb
bouncing

between mirrored walls
hopeless,

immortal,

not unhappy

three LIVE THROUGH

HOLIDAY

The ad
for the American moment

says, "Make
today famous."

(That little nobody!)

Bury her
under the foundation.

Rome did.

Have her wear that
seasonal

affective collapse
get up.

Keep an eye-
in-the-sky
on it.

GLARE

1

"It just goes so fast,"
says the receptionist,
your adverb here.

Indicate someone's feeling state.

Appeal to the senses.

INVASION

in yellow block letters,
second-story window.

2

The feeling is one.

The feeling is one of
following.

The feeling is one of following
a familiar trail

or legible sequence

between high walls,

between high walls
of noise

and glare

THE EYE

These brown piles
of stubble

hills

have failed.

They should be more

~

It should be difficult
but not impossible

to transmute
latitude

into a thought

a god could
hold.

~

Barred light:

dunes coming on
and on.

~

The eye, yes,
must move

to prevent
blank spots

from making themselves
known.

THE NEW ZOMBIE

1

I stare at a faint
spinning disc

in the black
endlessly

ready to pounce.

2

I actually say,

"I'm so sick
of zombies!"

3

Viral relics
in the genome?

Genes that switch
themselves off

and on,

unthinking
but coordinated?

4

Zombie surfeit.

Half-off zombie.

The best zombie
imitation.

Invisible zombie
hand

LIVE THROUGH

1

Fairy tales enchant the cast-off

one
cut out

of the third person.

2

You watch the storm
bear down on you
on television.

"I hope I never
have to live
through this
again."

3

Find Nemo
in the sea

of bodies,
ooze and muscle,

little flick-tail.

NOT

In the ongoing
concussion,

quick
Möbius strips

of bird song

fail to attach.

~

When the show comes back,
its theme song

no longer refers
to us.

~

"I

don't know

what you

think you

are, but"

~

A circle
has a center.

A circle is not
a face

KINGDOM

In the kingdom,
the open mouths

of flowers
aren't asking.

~

When you say she's "gone,"
you mean she's home.

She's sheets.

Cold
cirrus fingers.

Or she's expected soon
at the big air-space
gala.

~

In other words,
she speaks

and ruffled yellow throats
trumpet your arrival

at the Courtyard
Marriott

tomorrow

KINGDOM 2
(A POETICS)

"Sharon is Karen."
I never said that.

I just said,
"Get into the picture."

~

Phoneme clusters?

These things happen.

~

"Flock together,"
we say,

when we don't say,
"Opposites attract."

KILTER

Since I crop up
in sentences.

Since I can see
through your eyes.

Since I've been moved
into a mouse

in a cartoon
and then come back,

I can survive death.

⁓

This lateral
drift,

off-kilter

(as if one
saw double)

signals the approach
of sleep?

EXPRESSION

Give me your spurt
of verbs,

your welter
of pronouns

desiring to be spread.

Bulge-eyed, clear-
bodied brine-shrimp

bobbing to the surface.

I prefer
the hermit, trundling off

in someone else's
exoskeleton —

but we all
come down,

to self-love,
self-love which,

like a virus,

has no love
and has no self

AFTERLIFE

1

No longer needing sustenance,
butterflies
go batty around the flowers.

～

You call that nice?

I call it haiku.

Sugared tea.

2

Poisoned on the job,
the mad hatter becomes
a bit of nonsense
in a story
for lucky children.

BLESSED

1

This archipelago
of clouds
seen from above —

"isles of the blessed,"
yes,

though they aren't islands,

are uninhabited,

cannot belong
(be long),

is what I meant.

2

We are made up
of tiny rules.

The rules follow
themselves.

They try.

(We try.)

Nobody's perfect.

Every one is perfect.

CLEARANCE

If the clear wrapped
dark blue

lozenge
on each sink

at the W
with Bliss

inscribed on top
and bumps

like tire tread
on its bottom

is intended

~

A clear still
day, only

the butterflies
reel

as ever,

touching
on nothing

CLOUDLESS

You looked down by chance
and held my gaze
as if to show you weren't frightened,
though you must have been concerned
about what your eyes
might be able to express
and for how long.

Now one of us
would have to look away
as if disconcerted
or distracted.

But that was still
in the future.

Your eyes are a cloudless
blue-gray.

HOME

1

"May I be excused?"
is only used

when one has
finished eating

and is furious.

2

In truth, stillness kills us.

We depend
on the restlessness

of all that we don't see
for warmth.

3

What you always say:

pink and violet bands
upswept,

fading.

I hurry toward you,

turn the corner
and go home.

THE SCORE

1

One poet
slips out of

what each sentence
begins to say —

a magician
freeing himself

from the underwater
cage.

2

"They tell me I got this
Alzheimer's. I don't

know," he says
to the moderator,

as if doubt
were a way

to catch
one's fall

3

Folds
in the clear

curtains, columns
at dusk

scored by slant
ripples,

marked by stacked
apexes,

making some points

FALL

All summer florescence
scratches a vine's itch/

puckers
a vine's thick skin.

Serious buzz around it.

⁓

"I've fallen and I can't get up"
is funny

because we're not old

or we're not old yet

or not *really.*

⁓

Really is funny too.

⁓

This routine's
not empty.

It spells out
zero's location

in code.

⁓

Just like that
we're tickled

and we burst
open,

releasing drones

EXIT ROW

You will buy your life
as a series

of "experiences"

to which you
will belong.

Have a good flight.

       ~

Do you believe
in reproduction?

Do you think this
upland of clouds,

white buttes cut
by shadow canyons,

shapely and boundless

as the body
you were promised,

will reappear
after you're gone?

       ~

Boarding all zones at this time

DEEP TIME

In hide-and-seek
someone pretends to be

part
of his surroundings —

indistinguishable —

but is dug up
how many times?

Is found out
and eaten. No

is found
on a tape loop

showing every phase
and stunt,

allowing me
to pick out

this one
from the now

arriving now

DEVICE

The observer
is a device

(used by whom?)

to shrink time
to "the present."

~

Remember "escapism?"

~

In every mall,
World Market or Pier One

with their bins of
machine-dyed, glitter-drizzled

elephants.

LOUNGE AREA

Stiff stilts of herself.

Silver bag of herself
with turquoise gilt
midriff.

(Shake it but
no more will fit.)

Red lipstick line
between the folds —

precise —

opposite baby's soft
gurgling.

Have you lost your
passes?

Greeks pictured the afterlife
as an insipid version
of the world they knew.

But they couldn't
see this.

Two women,
with red mesh crests
atop white hair,

enter the lounge area;

one laughs, "I feel
like we should
say something."

NEW WAY

We punch our secret
code onto the image

of the earth as seen
from space.

~

We earmark trauma.

Looked at
in a new way,

trauma is.

~

Looked at from
upside down,

nothing has happened
yet.

~

Just put words
down, one

after the last.

~

Just get out
in time.

Of there

ABOUT THE AUTHOR

Rae Armantrout is a professor of writing and literature at the University of California, San Diego, and the author of twelve books of poetry, most recently *Just Saying* (2013), *Money Shot* (2011), and *Versed* (2010), winner of the Pulitzer Prize. An online reader's companion for this book is available at http://raearmantrout.site.wesleyan.edu.